Building with Magnets

Josephine Masterson

Rosen REAL READERS

Rosen Classroom™
New York

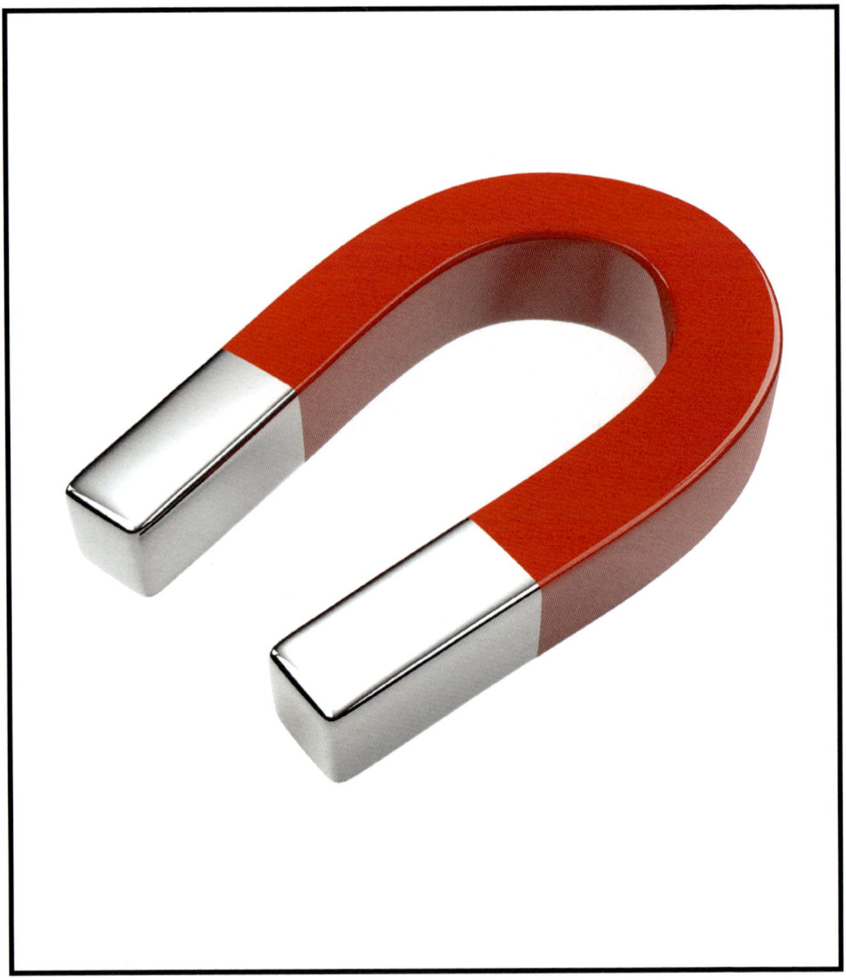

This is a magnet. It is an object that has a magnetic field. A magnet can attract or push away metal.

Magnets only interact with metals.

But not all metals interact with magnets.

Iron is a metal that does.

A refrigerator is built with magnets. Its door has a magnetic strip. It seals the door tightly to keep the cold air in.

A magnetic field is an invisible area around a magnet. It can also be temporary. One can be created by rubbing a magnet against iron.

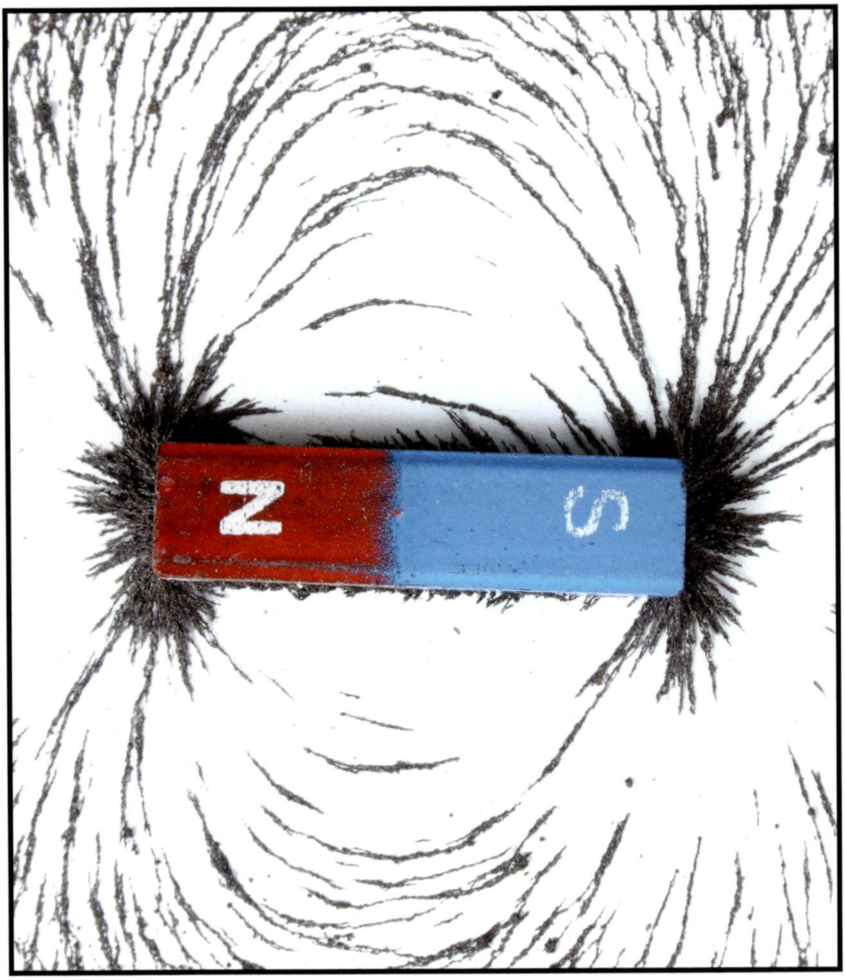

Magnets have two sides. They are called poles. One is the north pole. The opposite side is the south pole.

Magnetic fields are natural. Earth has a magnetic field. This is why a compass points to the North Pole.

A compass is a tool. It helps people navigate. It is built with a magnet. The pointer is attracted to the North Pole by Earth's magnetic field.

A computer is built with magnets. There are small ones inside a hard drive. Strong magnets work fast. They help you to open or save things faster.

An electromagnet is a type of magnet. Its field is controlled by electricity. Its magnetic field disappears when electricity is stopped. This magnet can move heavy metal in junkyards.

Vending machines are built with electromagnets. They can tell real coins from fake ones. Fake coins are attracted to the magnet. Real coins don't interact with magnets.

Glossary

compass A tool used for finding directions.

magnet A piece of metal that attracts certain other metals.

magnetic field A space where magnetic forces can be detected.

metal A substance that is usually hard and a good conductor of electricity and heat.